W9-AMU-315

Future COMMUNICATION

A CRESTWOOD HOUSE BOOK

CIP

LIBRARY OF CONGRESS CATALOGING IN PUBLICATION DATA

Abels, Harriette Sheffer.
  Future communications.

  (Our Future world)
  Bibliography: p.
  SUMMARY: Discusses innovations in communications which may alter many aspects of life.
    1. Communication--Juvenile literature. (1. Communication. 2. Inventions. 3. Technology) I. Schroeder, Howard. II. Vista III Design. III. Title. IV. Series.
P91.2.A24   001.51   80-16529
ISBN 0-89686-084-1 (lib. bdg.)
ISBN 0-89686-093-0 (pbk.)

INTERNATIONAL STANDARD BOOK NUMBERS:	**LIBRARY OF CONGRESS CATALOG CARD NUMBER:**
0-89686-084-1 Library Bound 0-89686-093-0 Paperback	80-16529

CRESTWOOD HOUSE

P.O. Box 3427, Hwy. 66 South
Mankato, MN 56001

FUTURE
COMMUNICATION

BY
HARRIETTE S. ABELS

23043

ILLUSTRATED BY:
VISTA III DESIGN

EDITED BY:
DR. HOWARD SCHROEDER
Professor in Reading and Language Arts
Dept. of Elementary Education
Mankato State University

GRAPHIC DESIGN BY:
MARK E. AHLSTROM

ART DIRECTION BY:
RANDAL M. HEISE

PHOTO CREDITS

Vista III Design: 23, 32, 33, 35
Bell Laboratories: 24, 36
Wide World Photos: 27, 39

In the past, predicting the future was an intellectual game. Sometimes the predictions came true. More often they didn't.

Today there is a new branch of science developing throughout the world. The people working in this field are called "Futurists." They are recognized as top experts in their fields. No one can say positively what the world will be like in the twenty-first century. But the Futurists are making some exciting predictions.

Communication means the exchange of thoughts and opinions between people. Today communication is of great interest to people everywhere.

Before we had either the telephone or the airplane we had to communicate with someone far away by writing to them. If a person in London had an argument with a friend in New York, it took weeks for their letters to go back and forth by ship across the Atlantic. By that time they had probably both forgotten what they were arguing about. Today that same person in London can pick up the telephone and be talking to a friend in New York a few minutes later, and the argument can be worked out right away.

Communicating in the future will be even faster than it is today and more important in our everyday lives.

Tomorrow's home may have one entire wall of electronic communication and computer equipment. If your "newspaper" comes on an electronic disk, you will be able to watch the news on your TV or just listen to it while you work.

TOMORROW'S NEWSPAPERS

Communication is going to get better, faster, and cheaper as we get into the twenty-first century. The biggest change in communication will probably be in the newspaper business. One futurist (person who studies the future) thinks the newspaper of tomorrow will be delivered to your home on a twelve-inch video disk. You will put this disk into

a slot in your television set. The stories that you read will have not only the printed words, but full-color photographs, moving pictures, and stereo sound effects. When your favorite baseball pitcher pitches a no-hit game and you read about it in your morning newspaper, you will also be able to see that final pitch and the wild excitement of his team-mates that follow it.

One form of this video disk already exists. It works by shining a thin beam of laser light onto a twelve-inch disk that looks similar to an aluminum-plated phonograph record. This laser needle reads signals put on the surface of the video disk in tiny hills and holes. This disk can hold up to one half hour of broadcast television. The disk not only has a picture signal but also two separate sound tracks so that the program can come through in more than one language.

A simple form of the electronic newspaper is already being used in Great Britain. A reporter writes his story on a video display terminal (a "printout" screen). As a button is pressed, the reporter's words can be read immediately in print on "teletex" sets all over Great Britain. The "reader" sitting in front of a television set tunes to a certain channel. A control box works off of that channel. It has many buttons. These buttons "turn the pages" of the Teletex. The

master "page" is an index. It shows all of the information to be seen on the electronic newspaper that
day.

Perhaps the reader wants to know what the
weather is around the world. He looks at the master
page. It tells him which button to push on the control box. You can actually see the electronic newspaper "flipping" its pages. When it reaches the one
on weather, it automatically stops.

Maybe someone would like to know what
specials are on sale in the downtown department
stores. That information is on another video "page."
Maybe another person would like to see a list of all
the soccer scores that week. By tuning in to that

"page," the whole report can be read. This service also tells the viewer what airline flights have seats available, and which stocks are selling best on the stock market.

Today these news stories are fed into British homes by the television service. In the future, with the video disk newspaper, every item of interest for that day will be available. Someday you should be able to read any newspaper in the world that you want to over your own television set. If you live in Los Angeles and want to see a copy of that day's New York Times or London Times, you will press a button on your television set and it will appear before your eyes. This kind of instant communication will be a giant step toward helping people all over the world to understand each other.

FUTURE LIBRARIES

Video disks will be used for many things besides your morning newspaper. One video disk could hold dozens of books from your bookshelf.

An entire thirty-volume encyclopedia could be easily placed on one video disk.

In libraries of the future, all of the information about one subject could be stored together on video disks no matter how it was available before. In other words, information on any subject, whether in fiction books, non-fiction books, from television programs, movies, or on records, could all be kept together.

Video disks can be used to keep the information together and also feed it into a computer. If a mini computer is added to the playback part of the disk, you will be able to have the machine preview the material and play back to you only the parts in which you are interested. It will also arrange the material for you in a different order than it appears on the original disk. This type of sorting and selection will be a useful new tool for education.

If you are studying for a test or exam, you could pick out the most important information and

Here is a schoolgirl of the future working on a paper for class. She can quickly get all the information on one subject with the touch of a button.

review it over and over again without having to go through all the printed material looking for what you want.

The libraries of the future will be based on a network system. All information will be stored in central computer buildings containing data banks.

Each building will contain information on a specific subject. Not only will public libraries be connected to these data bank places, but libraries in industry will also use them.

For instance, one data bank library center might specialize in gathering everything we know about food and food processing. A large cannery, or processor of food, might want to know the latest information on new preserving processes. It will be possible for their company librarian to get that information from the library center specializing in food information.

There are some subjects in which networking has already begun — motion pictures, for example. However, the importance of having all information in the same place has not been generally recognized.

There is a major change in the organization of libraries going on already. Rather than being places that merely gather information, libraries are now being seen as the place where that information is being carefully organized so that the person using the library can find it and use it more quickly and easily.

Outreach programs, programs that bring the library out of its own building and directly to the people, are already coming into use. We have pro-

In the future almost all communication will be by electronic combinations of sound and picture on a screen. This will be true of communication in education, business, and recreation.

grams that bring books to elderly people, the handicapped, prisoners, and even into small neighborhood centers in areas where there is no local library. In the future these programs will be greatly expanded. It will even be possible for some educational and cultural programs, run by the library, to be sent into the user's home by a delivery service or through the television.

Libraries can become centers for art and science

exhibits, craft displays, cultural exchanges, and even mini-museums.

The video cassette will also be an important part of the library of the future. The tapes are pre-recorded and can be used and checked out by the reader the same way as a book is today. At the present time there are only a few of the machines available to play back the video cassettes. In the future the library will be able to supply the video players to everyone. Until then, the video cassette can only be used within the library itself. Once the video disk comes into common use, anyone will be able to play movies, sports events, and re-created books on their own family television set.

The fantastic advances in disk technology will change forever the view of the public library as a quiet room filled with only shelves of books. The library of tomorrow will be out in the world.

ELECTRONIC MEETINGS

There is nothing that can take the place of meeting people in person. Shaking their hand and looking them straight in the eye, is the best kind of human communication. But this type of person-to-person meeting is not always possible. In the future there will be at least three electronic replacements to meeting in person. They are called video teleconferencing, computer teleconferencing, and audio teleconferencing.

With energy becoming scarcer, we will not be able to travel as much to have meetings with others, but we will be able to have meetings via video-conference hookups like this one.

Video teleconferencing means you can pick up your telephone and not only hear the person you are talking to, but also see them. Computer teleconferencing means holding a meeting by computers. It is done through a keyboard something like a typewriter. You can "talk" to each other right away, but all of the words are on paper. You can't hear each other. In audio teleconferencing two businesspeople speak on the telephone and can give each other written copies of whatever they are talking about right away by telewriting (sending printed information over telephone wires). The machines to do this are already in use.

PEOPLE AND THE MEDIA

Some futurists working in the field of sociology, the study of human society, see us living in a future worldwide "global village." They see the electronic media giving us a feeling of friendship for all the people of the world. When it is possible through that medium for a person in New York to

When we are able to share ideas in a personal way with people in other parts of the world, it will be easier to understand each other's problems.

meet electronically with a doctor in Africa or a farmer in China, today's problems between people will almost disappear.

In the field of government, all futurists agree that someday we will be one world with a one-world government. Electronic communication is a big step in that direction. Third-world and emerging nations will be on a more equal footing with our Western countries. National boundaries between countries won't mean as much.

Town meetings used to be an important part of small community life. In the future the hope is to have electronic town meetings, but with people from around the earth. This will encourage more people to take part in their government, at the local or national level, or even worldwide.

Cable television and satellites, along with computers and home terminals, will give us an electronic network that can greatly add to everyone's interest and sharing in government.

With this proper use of instant information we can be more productive and have less pressure on our environment. The big social problems of the world can be solved by easy communication between the world leaders. Floods, tornados and riots in faraway places will no longer be problems just for that local government. Help in the form of ideas, as well as emergency aid, can come from every part of the world. It will no longer take days to hear about a disaster in some far off part of South America or Africa. Once the world has instant communication, help and advice will be right there for everyone.

In the future a global communications network may link all countries. Operators will always be on duty to relay urgent messages to government and relief agencies.

(Top) **The satellite has already given us a whole new field of communication. In the future satellites will probably beam every kind of communication.** *(Bottom)* **Today "ham" radio operators rely on radio waves and favorable weather conditions. Tomorrow, they may broadcast through satellites and be guaranteed clear channel communication at all times.**

PEOPLE TO PEOPLE

Today a ham radio operator can talk to most places around the world. But a lot of what he picks up he gets by chance and by relying on the radio waves. These ham sets will get better and stronger. The operators will have much more control over them, because they will use satellites for clear channels.

Today we use the telephone as one way of communicating with other parts of the world, relying on operators to put through our calls. In the future, a mother who lives in California will be able to talk to her daughter in Bangkok, Thailand over her ham radio set without having to go through the telephone operator. For closer calls, citizens' band and mobile radios will be even better than they are now.

It will be possible for a wife in the suburbs to call her husband anywhere in the city to find out what time he will be home for dinner. While his wife is waiting the husband will call traffic control,

and when he hears how the traffic is on the high-
way, or if the electric busses are running on time, he
will tell her what time he will be at their front door.

Today our phone calls are sent mostly on land.
But very soon calls will go through satellites, giving
us a low-cost change from the many problems of
present-day telephone service.

Our telephone will probably always be the main kind of personal communication. But the telephones of tomorrow will be very different from the ones we have today. We already have fast communication by push button telephones in our own country. It is also possible to use this system to phone some other parts of the world. By the turn of the twenty-first century it should be possible to "dial" any big city on earth.

For years scientists have talked about television telephones, being able to see the person to whom you are speaking. This is now possible. However, to do this you must go to a special telephone company building and the people you are calling have to do the same on the other end. In the future every home will have this type of set.

In the beginning the set will probably be small and will sit right next to the telephone. Later there will be a large screen on which you will see the person you are talking to in life-size. It will also be possible to keep anyone from seeing you if you do not want to be seen. A teenage girl with her hair in curlers, who does not want her boyfriend to see her, will just push a cutoff switch and he will only hear her voice, just as we do today. When Alexander Graham Bell invented the telephone, he had no idea what his invention would lead to.

Even our mail system will be greatly improved. Computer mail services, and paying bills by electronic money systems, will change the mail service as we know it today. The United States mail service will move ahead to electronic mail. Our Zip Code system is the first step toward this. The Zip (Zone Improvement Plan) is read electronically and the mail automatically sorted.

It is quite likely that every home of the future may have phono-vision, letting you see the person you are talking with.

STUDYING ANIMAL COMMUNICATION

Many forms of animal communication are being studied today by scientists. It is hoped that by understanding how animals and other creatures communicate, we can better understand and simplify communication between human beings.

For many years scientists have been studying the dolphins. A dolphin is a member of the whale family. Whales are mamals, just as human beings are. They also feed their young with their own milk.

In some laboratories different kinds of sounds and forms of communication are being sent into space in search for other civilizations. One of the sounds being sent is that made by whales.

At the University of Texas, a behavioral psychologist is studying gerbils. Gerbils are a type of desert rodent somewhat like a hamster. Gerbils are also mammals. These gerbils are being studied in hopes they will help us better understand the structure of communication systems in mammals. The

two areas in which this study is concentrating are smells and sounds.

At the University of Texas they keep a constant gerbil flock of three hundred to four hundred animals. The gerbils live in "communities" and are never touched unless it's absolutely necessary. They are not treated as pets. Scientists try to keep their environment as close as possible to the natural environment of the Gerbils native home in Mongolia — this is so the Gerbils behavior patterns will not be disturbed.

The sounds the gerbils make are recorded on

high fidelity tape equipment. Some of their sounds can be heard, some cannot. The human ear can hear up to 20,000 cycles a second. But, gerbils talk much faster than that, approximately 32,000 cycles a second.

Once their sounds are recorded, the recording can be played at a lower speed to listen to the gerbils' ultrasonic speech. It is then possible, through a machine called a sonograph, to turn those sounds into a graph that can be seen.

Gerbils also communicate through smell. Of course this is much harder to measure. At times they communicate through releasing a special scent from a gland in the middle of their abdomen. They also have a gland called *Harder's Gland* that is wrapped around the eyeball. In the gerbil a canal leads from the Harder Gland to the tip of the nose. This releases a substance that cannot be seen. When the gerbil is grooming itself it spreads this substance over its face and then all over its body. This scent attracts other gerbils in the area and is connected to social position in the gerbil colony. It is possible to see this chemical released from the two glands under ultraviolet light.

Like other animals, gerbils always communicate for a particular reason. Cats do not meow and dogs do not bark just because they feel like it. All of

The strange little gerbil has ways of communicating that involve smell, as well as sight and sound.

Gerbils are mostly a community animal, and depend on communication to make things in the group run smoothly. As we study them we are able to learn how their community functions.

the things that animals do to communicate with each other take energy. They wouldn't do them if it weren't absolutely necessary.

The researchers have found that many of the gerbil signals are given to check and make certain that they're "working." In other words, they want to make sure that when they need to communicate with their fellow gerbils, the "lines" will be open.

Sometimes the researchers bring new gerbils into old gerbil communities. They find that at first the new animals do not understand all of the community members' signals, and the community members can't understand all of the newcomers' signals.

But as time passes and the new arrivals make themselves at home, their signals blend together. This is very much the same as two people meeting for the first time. Until people get to know each other, the first few minutes are often spent in meaningless talk.

It is possible for gerbils to change their way of communicating when the circumstances demand it. For instance, if a sudden breeze comes up and they have been communicating by sound, gerbils can switch to communicating by smell. By watching the animals it can be seen that these changes are made so they can clearly understand each other.

BEES

The most difficult, but specific "animal or creature" language yet discovered by man, is the language of bees. The language used inside the hive is used mainly by bee scouts. When they have found some nectar too far away to be easily found by smell or sight, and they want to share it with their fellow worker bees, they tell about it by doing a special dance on the honeycomb inside the hive. In this dance they quiver their abdomens by doing a strange "figure eight" maneuver. This dance was "translated" forty years ago by a famous Austrian zoologist. He discovered that the dance is filled with meaning.

The middle part of the figure eight tells the direction of the far-off nectar in relation to the direction of the sun. After the fellow bees have "read" the message several times and understood it, they actually go out and fly the course that the messenger bee has given them. The tempo of the dance tells the bees how far away the nectar is. A nectar close by is shown by fast dancing, and a nectar far away by slower dancing. The kind of nectar is also communicated in the dance by smell, since the

If you ever have the opportunity to look into a hive of bees, try to remember that many of their motions are communication to the other bees.

scout bee has picked up samples of it on her legs and body. During the middle portion of the figure eight dance, the bee hums quietly. The length of the time the humming lasts is also directly related to how far away the nectar is.

Since it is quite dark inside the bee hive the bee scout's message is not seen, but rather "read" in a type of braille by the sense of touch. The other bees gather around the dancing scout. They touch her with their shaking "feelers." They notice everything — how fast she is moving, what she tastes like, and above all, the exact angle of her path across the honeycomb. The fellow bees take in every detail and remember them so well that minutes later they can fly out practically right on target.

Because bees have such a highly developed language, it is possible for them to use it in governing themselves. When a hive decides to move to a new location, they start an operation called "swarming." Scout bees are sent out to look for a new site in a hollow tree, a hole in the ground, or perhaps a box. They then hold what might be called a nominating convention inside the old hive. Each of the scouts describes her favorite spot. She does this by a special dance, and tells how strongly she feels about the new location by the number of times she repeats the dance. Once the choice is nar-

When we harvest honey for our own use, we are really taking advantage of the bees' communication system. Because without good communication, the bees could not gather and make the honey.

rowed down to two or three places, the scouts go out again for a final look. Next they meet in a "high court" session where, by conversation and great discussion, they reach an almost unanimous agreement, and the hive flies to the new home.

How the study of communication between these creatures will help the human race is not yet known. However, as with most new information, the more we learn about other life, the more we understand ourselves.

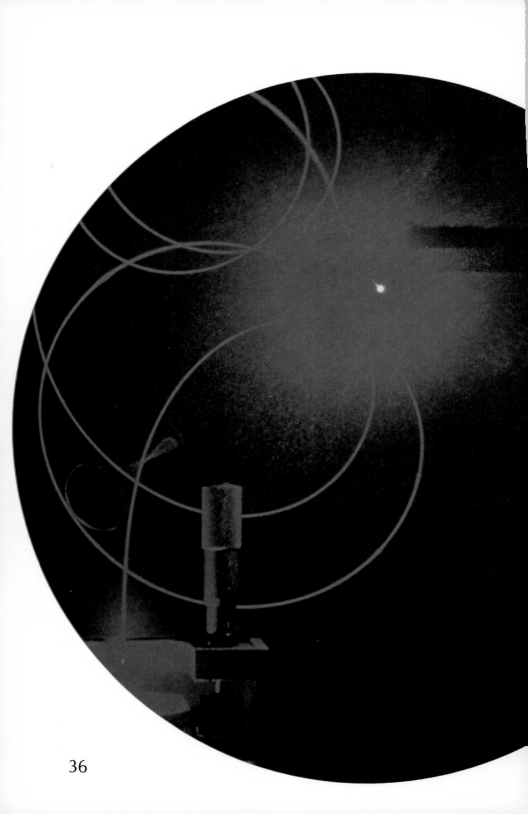

FUTURE TELEVISION

The greatest tool for communication in the future will be your television set. Today, except for a few educational television programs, television is used only for entertainment. Future television will be a center of entertainment, information, and education. These many uses of the TV set will be due to something called "fiber optics."

Fiber optics means sending a light beam from one point to another without letting it touch the open air. An optical fiber is a rough strand of clear glass. Each strand is then coated with another kind of glass that refracts (breaks up) in a different way. When a beam of light is sent through the inside glass, it travels through it with a very small loss of strength. The signal-carrying ability of these optical fibers is so great that one strand, less than the thickness of a human hair, can send as many as eight thousand different TV channels at the same time. These optical fibers can be bundled together to take the place of the copper wire cables

Here is a single strand fiber optic, which transmits light through its length even though it is bent and twisted several times. Many messages can be sent through a cable of these fine fibers.

now used in TV systems. These same fibers can also be used as telephone lines.

Fiber optics is the fastest spreading idea in the field of communication today. Every day new uses for it are being discovered and put to work.

Fiber optics has made the receiving ability of our TV sets endless. Instead of the six or seven VHF stations we have today, plus a handful of UHF stations, our sets will have an endless number of channels. This will make it possible for us to have the electronic newspaper with its many substations, and still have screen space for all the other uses that can be found for that set.

Entertainment will be far more varied than it is today. Along with our taped and pre-recorded programs we will see live-action filming of important events not only in our own country, but around the world. Today by satellite we see the Olympics every four years, or we see the coronation of the monarch in England once or twice in a lifetime. In the future, by satellite, we shall probably be able to view the important programs from every major country in the world every day if we want to.

Because we have developed the methods of global communication, we will soon see the best of sports and entertainment from all over the world.

TELEVISION AND EDUCATION

The big new use of television in the future will be in the field of education. Today we already have programs that teach us. You can even take a college credit course over the TV set. But future television education will be an entirely different system.

The big advantage of combining television with a computer is that you can interact with the machine in the learning process. Each student can work at his or her own rate, and go back over hard parts until they are fully understood.

Television education will be not only for school-age children but for adults who want to study a new subject or for an employee of a company who has to learn a new skill. The lesson will be shown directly on the TV screen.

Suppose you are studying math. You can play the same lesson over and over again if you are having trouble with it. With a set of dials or buttons you will answer the questions and your answers will be recorded on tape. If the answer is correct, you will know right away. If your answer is wrong, you will be told the right answer. You will also be shown how to do the problems correctly. There are TV sets that do this now, but they are very expensive and available to only a few people. In the future these lessons will be shown on family TV sets.

Some futurists feel we will always have schools and classrooms, the same as we know them today. Other futurists see the time, perhaps 100 or 150 years from now, when there will be no school buildings, no individual teachers, and everything will be taught over the TV screen.

The TV Screen itself will not be the small twenty-one or twenty-seven inch box that we have today. It will be common to have screens permanently fixed in one or more of the walls in your home. They will cover an area perhaps as big as six feet by six feet. The effects of a TV screen of this size on our minds will be enormous.

Imagine seeing a football game or a baseball game with the players appearing life-size right in front of your eyes. Watching a movie would be almost like watching a stage play in person. As the actors move about the screen, they will seem to be in the same room with you.

This huge TV screen and the speed with which it will bring news and information into our lives should also affect us in other ways. When we see such tragedies as an apartment house fire with its

TV which is almost life-size is not very far away for the average homeowner. When you watch a football game, you will feel like you are right in the middle of the action.

victims, or a terrible automobile accident, perhaps it will teach us to be more careful in all areas of our everyday life. There is a big difference between reading about such things in your daily newspaper, or seeing them on your tiny TV screen of today, and seeing them in life-size images in your own living room.

(Left) Communication is the key to our becoming "one-world" and knowing all persons as our friends. (Right) Perhaps in the next century communication will have brought us to one-world government, so we could stand up and say the "Pledge of Allegiance to the World."

If there is ever another major war and it is seen on this giant screen in front of our eyes, maybe for the first time in the history of man we will all stand up and shout, "No! No more! Man has grown beyond this type of animal behavior."

The TV system of the future can be used for good or for evil. A shouting political leader, with a fascinating way of wrapping his silky words around us, could use this future TV system to rule the whole world. It will be up to all of us to see that this wonderful new tool is used for good, and not for evil, in the centuries ahead.

GLOSSARY
OF TERMS USED IN
FUTURE
Communication

AUDIO TELECOMMUNICATION — Holding a group meeting by telephone and instant computer readouts.

COMMUNICATION — The exchange of thoughts and opinions.

COMPUTER TELECOMMUNICATION — Holding a group meeting through an exchange of computer messages.

FIBER OPTICS — Sending light beams through very thin glass strands.

FUTURIST — A scientist who studies the future.

LASER BEAM — Stimulating high energy atoms by light.

SOCIOLOGY — The study of people and how they live.

STEREO (Stereophonic) — Three dimensional sound.

VIDEO DISK — A thin, round object which contains large amounts of information.

VIDEO TELECOMMUNICATION — Holding a group meeting by video-telephone.

Harriette Sheffer Abels was born December 1, 1926 in Port Chester, New York. She attended Furman University, Greenville, South Carolina for one year. In addition to having her poetry published in the Furman literary magazine, she had her first major literary success while at the University. She wrote, produced and directed a three act musical comedy that was a smash hit!

At the age of twenty she moved to California, where she worked as a medical secretary for four years. In September, 1949, she married Robert Hamilton Abels, a manufacturers sales representative.

She began writing professionally in September, 1963. Her first major story was published in **Highlights For Children** in March, 1964, and her second appeared in **Jack and Jill** a short while later. She has been selling stories and articles ever since. Her first book was published by Ginn & Co., for the Magic Circle Program, in 1970.

Harriette and her husband love to travel and are looking forward to their annual trip to Europe. While travel doesn't leave much time for writing, Harriette does try to write at least something every day. When at home a sunporch serves as her office, but she confesses that most of her serious writing is done while stretched out on her bed.

The Abels have three children - Barbara Heidi, David Mark, and Carol Susan, and three dogs - Coco, Bon Bon, and Ginger Ale.

OUR FUTURE WORLD